A WOMAN KNEELING IN THE BIG CITY

A
WOMAN
KNEELING

IN THE
BIG CITY

Elizabeth Macklin

W. W. NORTON & COMPANY

NEW YORK / LONDON

For Marjorie
(after hearing of
you for years —
finally meeting)
With warm regards
Elizabeth Macklin
4·8·98

The text of this book is composed in Perpetua, with the display set in Huxley Vertical.
Composition by PennSet, Inc., Manufacturing by the Courier Companies, Inc.
Book design by Michael Chesworth.

Library of Congress Cataloging-in-Publication Data
Macklin, Elizabeth.
  A woman kneeling in the big city / Elizabeth Macklin.
    p.   cm.
    I. Title.
  PS3563.A318737W6   1992
  811'.54—dc20   92–3388

ISBN 0-393-03400-3

W.W. Norton & Company, Inc., 500 Fifth Avenue, New York, N.Y. 10110
W.W. Norton & Company Ltd., 10 Coptic Street, London WC1A 1PU

1 2 3 4 5 6 7 8 9 0

My thanks to the Ingram Merrill Foundation, with whose help this book was completed. And
to the following magazines and their editors:
CANTO ("A Woman Paging Through Seed Catalogues," "Having Unwrapped a Recent Present"),
LYRA ("A Translation of Love in Public"), MINNESOTA REVIEW ("A Woman at Ground Zero"),
THE NATION ("Interpreters in One Language"), NEW ENGLAND REVIEW ("A Woman Revising
Her Scrapbooks"), THE NEW YORKER ("Three Views of a Woman Inhaling," "The Bird in the
Dooryard," "A Married Couple Discovers Irreconcilable Differences," "A Woman Picks Up
the Habit of Anger," "The Unruly Thoughts of the Dog Trainer's Lover," "A Woman Kneeling
in the Big City," "All Over," "Brecht Backstage: The Good Master," "Where Inside Is Dark
or Light," "Seeking to Account to a Fisherman Thief," "Chiding the Very-God," "Instructions:
Early Epiphanies," "Ornament in a Port City," "The Sorry Creatures in This Countryside,"
"The Two Scenes in Color," "Surface Tension," "Our Fall," "Looking to Console the Maker,"
"Reassurance in a Hot Summer," "I Imagine Back," "At the Creek Edge," "The Only Child
Sends a Gift to Her Mother," "By Daylight," "More," "At the Classics Teacher's," "Love Song
to the World Leaders," "We Love It No End," "I Fail to Speak to My Earth, My Desire,"
"Proofreading My Father's Retina," "For Chéri," "The Watches," "The Nearsighted"), THE
PARIS REVIEW ("Brooding," "There Is Still Water," "What Now"), POETRY ("Leaving One of
the State Parks After a Family Outing"), SOUTHWEST REVIEW ("In Tompkins Square Park," "A
Confession of Lies"), THREEPENNY REVIEW ("Two Bear"), VERSE ("Now the Heroine Weakens
and Speaks"), THE YALE REVIEW ("A Field Guide to Lesser Desires").
And especially to Mary Norris, Mary Painter, Alastair Reid, Alison Rose, and Edward M.
Stringham, for their great help over the years.

For
Edward Carlyle Wood
and
Margaret Herkenratt Wood

CONTENTS

In Color

A WOMAN KNEELING IN THE BIG CITY

Instructions: Early Epiphanies

What to do: First you put your hand on her arm
on a weekday morning, coming out of the subway.
Nothing flies up from the street that shouldn't—
not newspapers, not trash. The island's becalmed,
dazzling: mica is caught in the sidewalk,
it's ten o'clock, too early in the year for shade.

Test: Does the pavement tremble? Trains pull away
under you and the ground. Cross calmer streets to
edge by Chinatown, bright-red boxes
of snow peas and white-leaf cabbage. Stay
on the corner a moment, tighten your grip.
Try to get over it—your shaken street scene.

On East Broadway, face east, close your eyes
against tractor-trailer soot, against bleach-light.
When you open them, first see shambles, pickup, delivery,
black-crate foreign lettering, wood chips, coin-size
buying and selling. You'll soon find a cafeteria. Take
her in. The clatter may startle her. Take her anyway.

The point of all this is breakfast on a brown tray.
Show her the slices of challah. *Do you want this?*
The eggs. *This?* All the choices are gold and white
in the middle, brown on the edges, zigzag, serrated.
Sit down at a table, have your vision.
It will take some minutes. Finish eating. Pay.

You may have left her bewildered; she may look at you
warily, or shake her head. On a twelve-o'clock horn-blazing
sidewalk say loudly "Now!" or "It's nothing!" Take her
hand. Charm her completely. Put her at ease again. Now.
Remember what brought on the vision. Work very hard.
It could happen again some morning.

IN
THE
BIG
CITY

All Over

All of a sudden one year, we seemed to be dying
in droves, in whole or in part. This one lost a breast
as if it were a child. That one's head filled dark to bursting
like a stranger blackjacked, over and over. One simply died.
There were those of us forced to straitjacket maddened color,
or helpless desire. Twelve of us woke up
robbed, in varied ways. All of us watched our breath
blacken the air before us on cold days. All over,
we seemed to be dying.
The eyes of one of our own fell to tatters
and stopped reading, or seeing.
And drunks came down from the bars with their arms flung wide,
calling, *"This way—this way."* And held out their trousers
like children's nightclothes, for us to climb into
and sleep, or cry.

Our Fall

1988

It's not only just beginning to be unwarm.
We've found neither love nor money for a good

eight years. The paper on fire in the gutter was
not money. I don't know where we are; it is not like

jail. For a moment, let's try to sit inside
the garden; no, nothing is for us behind those bars.

The pavement runs house to house, is hard
to walk on. It sparkles with glass, mica, and no

spare change. The unlined pockets are the ones with holes
now. Like a perfect seamstress, I will tell you it is all

my fault. I believe our walls must be brown paper.
Anyone can hear us struggle at any time.

Chiding the Very-God

I can't imagine medicine given me
by your hand. Maybe a human hand
holds a spoon to my lips—round bowl
full above a careful palm—or places
a small pill on my tongue.
The hand may move by reason of you.
Just now I'm speaking to no one.
I can see how the gray-blue spoon might
shine, the near hand move, move, and move.
How the hand's held out, to say, "Now,
here." Pity and sickness or grace, cure—
each received for all the mysterious reasons.

A Field Guide to Lesser Desires

1

Straight as a line, as a drawn bead,
as jaybirds pulled to a window roof
in a bare borough, we've come to breathe
for our supper: seed hissing onto a tin tray,
a meeting of scattered needs—
food.

2

Like singsong addicts, we lose all
sense of time by the clock: too short
is what to call this year,
and "long" is the word for
minutes.

3

The great caretaker of these poor pigeons
lets the cats at them. I'd say our shelter
shelters like a high wind: desire everywhere,
like feathers. If it were warm, if we were only
hummingbirds, we'd drink
nectar.

4

And as if we foretasted more than water,
and a tissue-thin message wrapped every
limb—at last, "Come here, I
need you"—we bend to fall to the
least tree. What we will do here is just
sin.

Looking to Console the Maker

A potter fragile as porcelain is reading this,
fragile and cool as shatter gone back to slip.

In a room where a wheel turns and clay thins
someone who has to start from scratch is starting in.

Bright with blue paint and unlikely lines,
a wet gray shell holds still for a new brush.

The potter tries another color and another touch.
A marsh bird builds among rushes, to that design.

A potter breakable as china is firing clay:
the kiln is white with heat, the surface waves

with heat; the blue and thin-white glaze
is cool as water. Who holds the vase?

What Now

is coming from the hunters' woods
with open hands, allowing

everything new. What now seeks needs
to satisfy. Each bough

sheds gold scent on those hands in beads
of resin. Each wet shower

of clean snow off the branches fills a riverbed
for the thirsty. No, no drought

this year. What now takes care. What now has made
a lasting truce with the wide sky. How

can it come about? A slow, vast generosity has loaded
the earth with treasure and what now.

A Confession of Lies

No, it isn't needed: this blue sky, the two exact trees
Where they are—green ash, blue pine. The seas can rise
To within an inch of the buildings but will not,
Ever. For now, like them, my words can be trusted.
There is no need for a doubt. We will not die.
We cannot keep the woods from receding north
To a cooler horizon. Red, white, and yellow
Trash will escape our hands to go into the water.
A glowing, new coal will escape our lips and go down
Through time in the water, to come up a cool, gold
Drink. The truth: We aren't eager to die. We
Turn all our acts to good. We think and desire
Alike. Whatever we start we complete. We don't
Let our anger loose. All earth
Is as wide and dear and clean as when I was small.
Whenever I lie, I tell a truth.

Ornament in a Port City

The wind—and there is a wind—might as well be
my body against my body: all day, heat;
and it hasn't rained. Anywhere else

the heavens or sky would be black by now,
or black-blue. Here the buildings get so dark
the air is white beside them, holding up its near-clear

load of water. Trash trees
send live pollen into the air until it's
hard to breathe. This under sparse gold windows,

and by a fenced playground. Four shut stores, a doorway,
then a man has set earrings in a dark cloth square
in a square of light. In all the colors,

as if to say: "Anything that can be pierced
and strung on a wire." A chalk-melon pair,
meaning coral; a mirror one. A turquoise,

or something meant for turquoise.

More

Sidewalks for thirty blocks, more,
in the city. I think every smell
in the world has a place here:

greens beside grocers'; cardboard
like broken books soaking in water;
exhaust, both diesel and gasoline.

Fried meat and frying fish leap
in a hot mist. Then, near the end,
there is grass and sycamores,

a park like a back yard—
leaves in town. Make it plain:
it's hard to desire diversity.

That's what there is. All people lie
whichway on benches in squares,
ill-sheltered in doorways,

away from the street. It's easy, like
breathing. We can't stand to say how
foreign we are, so we say we are not.

I'm longing to sit down to supper,
where often there's choice. Each smell
can taste like a million, cooking.

Steam contains worlds, in the flying
water. Sometimes there's nothing.
And found bread will do. Then

chances lie furred in a dark den
inside, to say, *"Everywhere."* Every
flat surface a stove or a breadboard,

a table laid ready. Hunger is
just lack of sleep spread thin.
A meal is no more than a bed.

Every desire is alike an addiction
that lives in a hive in the body,
hidden as honey. We say we are not

when we are; we walk for hours.
Hungry, we swear we are not, hands high.
We say we are not, when we are.

Reassurance in a Hot Summer

The woman and the dragon in the sand-colored room
are here forever, are here forever.
Regards, regards forever from one of the two.

The dragon the color of flame, the woman of salt
in a roomful of air, a room of sand:
the dragon is long and fierce, the woman is tall,

their arms are chalk or foam. They hold each other.
They feed one another sugar or flame.
Too sweet and hot and blind are the words they utter.

They and their days are covered with sand and water.
Merged and turning to bottle-green glass,
they hold us dear as wine as the days grow hotter.

Where Inside Is Dark or Light

I am left alone in the city-tree dark outside.
Gray tracks gathered together in a navy field,
a flock of clouds make the night sky
over the broken courtyard something to see.
A measure of sky falls down between
two tall buildings, too, nearby. A woman, my
friend, is talking on the phone inside, behind me.
Every building around fairly breathes
with windows. They aren't darkened or lighted
at random. It's a choice: to lean forward,
to try to see; to lean back and admire the sky.

I could be, I believed, in any one of them,
darkened or light, the glass seen through
like tears come into my eyes, from
grief or joy. The smell of the trees comes
up like asters or pollen to the new, low
rooftop. In a window someone, some
one young woman, curves her long cool
neck to drink, too, lost leopard at a stone-
hemmed pool. Beside her, there is a round family.
My girl-voiced friend keeps talking away home.
Here a loving sky's come out a deep clear blue.

15

A Woman at Ground Zero

Time to time,
I feel a knotted sun,
solar plexus, rise
like the underside
of the city
overturned:

here are the emptied hollows
where water ran;
there, brokenhearted cuts
for unearthed cables
stripped of our copper current
and our voices;
underneath, the twisted rails
of complicated trains

that couldn't get there from here.
And I think, So it was all
topweighted?
built too fast by no one—
in short, on sand—
and so fell through?

I forget the facts,
the jackhammers and drivers.
The slow-swung crane:
the culvert lowered into the pit,
daylight moving shoals of orange
helmets over it. I forget the hands
shading the eyes that long to see

a wide, completed
avenue
with caravans
of flagged and yellow trucks
parading between tall trees, a joyride,
barreling over the worksite—

because that has not yet happened.
And because that has not happened
I see a scavenger wheel, alone alive,
over an upturned city,

and find a hard, unhopeful woman in my chest
from time to time.

Love Song to the World Leaders

When I lie back it's as if you said to me
"Once there was an island" and at once there's nutmeg
in every house and I am in a hammock in the green
trees, and prides of grasses are roaring.
When I lie back it's as if I thought
you wouldn't dare to shake me or let me
fall, as if I thought your arms so strong they'd
hold forever, rope bridges over crevasses: there
is a pool down there, and blue-green water
in bare-sand rocks.
It's as if I were not dizzy.

And when I get up, I can see the whole
black island in sunlight sink in the sea,
tilting. A spray flies up when it's under.
It's as if you'd told me "Once there was an island
and so forth, so on," already lying.
It's almost as if it had never been.

How the Faithful Court the Impulse

I believe books when you show them to me.
I believe bound, paper books.

I believe acts
when you take them up and lay them out.

When you lay them down and stroke their hair,
stroke their foreheads,

I believe in
acts. I believe what is foreign to me. This

act—this blind, injured saint—lies
before me like a healer awry.

I believe
its pulse: it is an animal like me.

I believe in its wet-dark hair. I believe
its anger.

I believe I can nurse it
back to health. It's the most I can do.

It may, to be sure, be a poor, partial
creature.

At times I'm afraid when I read its
heart. I hold to its grand, whole anger.

In Tompkins Square Park

1984

I thought they were doing something European—
something so free that on all the plains, purpled
hills, rills it had never been seen
here.
        I thought they had knelt; had
fallen onto the wide green city lawn; had
propped themselves in the sidewise light
on one arm, gone straight into conversation.

I thought they had thought—long, hard,
long—through all the results of their actions,
had drawn each blade of foreseeable pain,
bitten its white-green end, and only then drawn
conclusions.
                I went on watching till late at night
in my mind's highly imaginative eye, and believed
they were doing something European.

Interpreters in One Language

The harbor's the dull side of foil today.
If this were theatre, there would be muffled thunder.
The sky is perfectly gray, a clouded plate.
Staten Island is all black trees, Manhattan's
built on something like pyrite—a fool's slate—
asphalt, and concrete. Not far away, a ferryboat's passing,
freighting something like goldenrod from painted borough to
                                                    borough.

When speaking a foreign language, everything
is unreal. Anything could have been said; conversation
has no basis in fact. A word, born somewhere else,
reminds its listener of nothing intentional. Longing itself
knows just how sketchy it is. It's the best of unspeakable
paintings: here is the work of years of nearsighted souls
who came across so clearly on paper.

The question today is jellyfish in the river—why
transparent beings are not invisible. Why would
somebody want power? All the speakers longed
for something that they could control, for things
to go perfectly right for a change. No nasty surprises.
By the end of the speeches, the harbor the way it is,
all of us came to see how much we longed for surprises.

There Is Still Water

There are still hammers, aren't there,
somewhere, and bricks dried in brick kilns?

Work has stopped for the winter,
never to start again.

Or it goes on behind closed doors,
till you see no sign of the seasons.

Pride seems to go with the baked loaf:
Tin rows of pans move like soldiers

into the ovens. The bakers wear masks.
Even here there is time enough to slip a word in.

All that we eat was fashioned
by someone.

Now snow follows the line of the railings,
as if to prove winter. Across the avenue

an I-beam flies on a crane line.
No other motion there captures the eye:

this newest building will be done that soon,
built, like the evangelical world, by no one.

There is still water, a river,
moving down either side of the city—

or does it disappear, like a right, too,
when no one is watching?

Elsewhere craftsmen have uncovered their faces,
have made themselves known, and none too soon.

As if spring. Work as they tell you.

I Fail to Speak to My Earth, My Desire

Having set my heart on you, I remove it
and set it aside. You my desire,
my table, my solid ground, my own true
surface. A mouse in any corner may try
to come out. A wind may cool and blow
us askew. You my desire are not my
property. You may not ever be so.

You my love, my world. Now, have I set my heart on
you? A trace, a kiss, a print, a small brown
scratch: Do you have a clue? Kind as you are,
I am proud or—   Nothing in the whole great house
will show where the heart is now. Nor
will the mouse find comforting crumbs. As if, my ground,
I were still waiting to be shown what it is I am for.

Seeking to Account to a Fisherman Thief

See this fish flipping around, hand-sized, silver to
gold? See the caught suns scaled down in its sun-
fish sides? Look, here's the shade
under the unpaid dock, dark and smooth, where you
threw him back. But, look, here's the grass-green
shade on the shore, where you keep him.

And see this fish flying up into the shallow sky
to eat, inches? See that heavier weight, cast
high into the spyglass sky, though—miles? Down here,
a held, then skipped, then lost silver dollar's as
dear as strong drink: elixir. There where
a dollar is trash are rivers of them.

At the Classics Teacher's

You gave us phlox, blue-rose, burst on the marble
table in the back yard, the word in bloom like the sound
fire makes when it leaps—*phlox*—into being.

Our friend has gone to sleep, blue-white, this evening
on the black grass. Beside him, a pine-green spotlight falls
where, torchlight, the kerosene shines. There are no clouds.

Cloud-gray phlox in front of us, though. Not everything's lost,
not everything's shaken. Your clean, safe-surrounded house
has a back door into its garden. Your pinks have blue-gray

leaves. Your broken porch has a strong false floor. There's a
                                                        place
to hide just behind the trellis covered in larkspur. Across
two rivers and fifty miles, our tiny great city is crowned

in acres of gray-pink light. It smokes, it could be on fire,
with all its division and anger. Night is making it loud
even now, but we don't hear it. In the garden tonight we're
                                                        turned

to another city—cities: How the ex-queen Hecuba cried *oimoi*

over

captured daughters and two dead sons. How Troy was flicked

from its

pyre of ashes and became Rome. How S. Weil proved that

hounding

force, like hounding charity, turns its object to stone. Our friend

turns over and wakes up, mentions the stars. He laughs aloud:

"Found

it." He's forgotten, he says, the whole sky except for the Bear,

the Dipper, after all this time. "Look." We look, we gaze,

we stare

at the ones we see and the ones we cannot see. You laugh,

and send

us looking for Cassiopeia on her visible chair. We allow

as she might be somewhere. Those poor sailors, believers,

swimming

cousins, their stars arranged into patterns they could

understand—

how they longed, like fossils in water, to stay in mind,

their impression buried in mud of a certain kind.
We debate their conjugations, their words like men and women,
yoked to sense. How is it that the word "to bear," as in pounds

of burden, in the present (*fero*) was not at all like the word
"to bear" in the past (*tuli*), the "perfect"? We do not know,
but we can guess. And how are the slaves who bear our peace?

If we do not know, we do not know. We can guess, at the
very least.
You were positing how to move a kind of knowledge into the
world,
how Virgil, off on his farm in wartime, reported the sounds

of bees, soil, reaping. You stepped indoors for something: "Wait
right here." Our friend (you should know) said some words
about
you. Then you came out with water, ice, sugar, lemons.

Catullus and his supper guests who had to bring their own
provisions
didn't drink like this. All nose and mouth, we inhaled, we drank
what only in your buried garden tastes whole and round.

The Sorry Creatures in This Countryside

Under some rushing, creaking trees are
three little bobcats, trapped. They tell me,
"We're trapped."
                              Sharp steel words
in springing phrases of birth: they say these
trapped them. They cry out loud and complain.

Under the rushing trees I tell them, "Yes,
I believe you. I was raised
to believe you. I'm trapped, too."

Who can imagine now how boys came
out of a wolf den to rule like men, or if rules
were the same then?
                              My free-spoken bobcats,
trapped, believe that the gods have changed
since then. They favor their bruised little paws

and are scared to move.
I favor their short, sharp claws
but am scared to move.

IN
THIS
COUNTRYSIDE

A Woman Revising Her Scrapbooks

First I'm rewriting my small white-leather-
covered babyhood, where I dream damp hair
under cellophane tape deepens to a child's
sienna-curled brushstroke, like straw burning
into dark ash. The binding is now sky-blue
Italian paper, designed all over with gold-
rose whorls, and new fingerprints.

I paste in other snapshots, with pinked edges:
the color of green under not yet dead elms
in some older country, unfallen before disease;
a cotton sheet; a new, rolling, steamboat father,
his tiny yellow-wrapped girl caught up
in midair by a pressing mother's camera.
And breast milk gleaming on a napkin.

My meals were not so filling, not so long-planned:
I was raised one of inconceivable offspring,
washed clean, fed on bottles of dry, white milk
sucked in scattered houses across a dismantled nation.
We were flung home, out of reach as lost grain,
far from the rows of old family, our mothers
all making desperate penciled notations.

I color those sketches over, in another language,
or farther south—the entry in brown penmanship,
my first, lost steps across uneven tiles to a carved
table, touching all my aunts. Or sew in lace, leafy
as the underside of formal gardens, hemming foreign
christenings, promised to schools of nuns
down a narrow, satchel, cobble alley.

The grand bright family is folded inside
the middle pages, complete with priests at table,
for a wedding. My own hand jumps, dark, slight,
showing off light-blue transparent signatures:
a fourth generation. We sit down to eat
game hunted in low north foothills by my father,
thrush fed on elderberries, thrush tasting of
elderberries, hare tasting of wild sorrel.

Leaving One of the State Parks
After a Family Outing

The grass was the green of parades when we'd leave,
loading the trunk of the car in the summer evening.
The trees were all elms, shadows immense, and our thirst
was waiting to go somewhere for ice cream.

You would say *Do this, Elizabeth,* and I would do it
as if it were a game, on afternoons like that: I'd
spread wet towels on the back seat, go and fetch things,
put Mama's purse in the corner, close the door, "click,"

like two people kissing. Then I always said *Can we coast
today? Can we?* Mama would mention, Carl, it was illegal;
but you put the car in neutral, in the shade facing the
long hill—released all the brakes.

In the back I would make small pushing motions
against the front seat, as if a little girl like me
could move an automobile. The car would sit, edged
with the chance of falling, then, slowly, begin to roll.

How I loved you then, your hands on the wheel in the
strong almost twilight, as you did something just for me
at last. The park lilac bushes pass us in shadow
as though about to stop. We falter, come up to

a slight rise. Then we begin the wild controlled descent,
silent as bicycles but weighing tons. The elm-tree
shadows fly over the hood and down behind; you begin
to brake for the main road approaching. *Had enough?*

Then of course you turned the ignition over, eased us
down to stop in second gear. We went from there
for ice cream or for root beer, without having
heard the question answered: *No!* if I could've known

how to say it. *It's never enough.* I want to go down
with you forever, without anger, pulled by the weight of the car
in the steady descending silence, always just before sunset,
rolling through leaves, in some perpetually loving motion.

The Bird in the Dooryard

At my mother's house there is a bird that sings
all night, loud, from deep inside the juniper,
from dusk through the black to the gray to the
light gray to the gray-blue—clear as water or clear
as gin. The following night it begins again.

To go to sleep in my mother's house you must be
stone-deaf, out cold, or covered with glass or
water. You must have no ears. Only open archways
separate the rooms, and the wind collects in pools
in your very corner. High-pitched and varied,

true, the bird's singing in the juniper outside
my mother's door will give you no peace. Gin through a
straw, possibly. Or notes of high drunkenness, tippling
                    down through the branches.

Three Views of a Woman Inhaling

There was a month when I looked every day
for what it was that smelled like this:
the shade in the burning whitewashed alley,
pungent and filling as silo grain; sand-colored
stucco shadowed by leaf-dapple. I would walk
with laundry piled in white folds on my arm, lean
over the banked glowing bushes, and smell for it.

In late summer, that same year, I was struck again
by the mysteries. One noon hour, on the steps of
an airplane, the smell was thick in the air of Spain.
Every shadow was black, sharp-edged on the macadam;
you could be sure the smell had cast them.
The smell there was shady—filled with earlier days
and white cotton—and it came out of nowhere.

Four stories above the Brooklyn courtyards
on a cool summer day, another year, I leaned out
to take clean linen off the line, snapping the sheets
hard in the city wind. Inside, bread lay covered by cloths.
The warm crust inside smelled of knife-trees.
When sycamore leaves snapped taut on the line,
knives flew like pigeons down to the pavement.

Having Unwrapped a Recent Present

There are more frightening gifts that could be given
than hours of lying back all still and wild,
night-bells ringing like sheep in groves of olives,
aware of the sea around a fruit-tree island.

There are more frightening gifts—but not too many:
sometimes love draws up a net of fishes
that move like minnows caught and caught again,
poured on deck. Black nets make black additions.

So, even given a gentle meal of olives,
hands on breasts, and fishes, or full kisses,
I've somehow netted darkness—called up, living
for no apparent reason. The nets are stiffened.

The meal goes on like trout in summer shallows;
nets hang, just so, over our moving shadow.

A Married Couple Discovers
Irreconcilable Differences

We are riding through the city one night,
under trees. Hawthorn hedges flower
along the park drives.

Sitting on the passenger side,
I cup my hand in the wind outside the car.
I hold my hand to my ear:

What were you saying?
My hand gets colder.
The side of my face

near the window doesn't feel real;
the other side is hot
in the face of reason.

I agree with you, wholly.
But the hand out there
curves around with the wind,

draws it in,
filled with tree breath.
I can hardly speak.

For Chéri

Here are all these women getting all unthinking
into costume, backstage at the theatre—*tes sœurs*—

under duress in feathers.
Now we disguise our eyes—no, our

desire—again! Shadow as aquamarine and gold as
painted boats in a harbor,

underwater. Sea-green paint aslant, or—
daring—coral.

　　　　　　Wool dressing gowns, of course—for air
at the stage door. Aren't there always three reasons?

One is a master. One a game. Then one boy, in an
alleyway. Sit down now and eat on the iron stairs,

finish in agitation. Now come inside,
get ready. Now let the baize door slam.

Soon we will act
like girls again.

The Unruly Thoughts of the
Dog Trainer's Lover

Into the wheat-thrown fields we lead
the leashed dogs, the well-trained hounds;
they leap to mind through the weedy
Queen Anne's lace. He orders them, "Circle round,
round." I'm a willing believer.

They run together—gray water, tail to mouth—
in wheeling stories. Their frilled jaws
can hold eggs, live rabbits, our wrists. At his brief sign
they make no sound. I am properly awed.
Their paws wear great rings of grass down.

He wields the commands "Sit," "Stay"
like a stick and a thorn. He can say "Fetch" or "Leave":
they scatter in ashen explosions. Waving
devoted tails like prayer flags, they look for reprieve to me.
I shrug. He gestures "Heel." They come through meticulous

                                                    paces.

I'm here to reward us all when we lie down,
to roll over into the pasture hay, to carry a sack
of marrow bones tight in my loose
hand. I wear his clothes like khaki
fatigues in the afternoon. He stands his ground.

I hear mongrel packs have taken the roads upstate,
attacking deer at will. But we will go to the kennel show
for blue, snapping ribbons. The fairgrounds will shake
under the truck. He'll call the dogs: "Go slowly, hounds.
I said go slow." We all may have made a grave mistake.

A Woman Paging Through Seed Catalogues

I'm going to plant elderberries from the catalogues
this year, because I was never allowed to plant
elderberries.
I plan to dig carefully around the roots
and prune the branches back in the right season,
though I don't much care for their dark fruit.

In our back yard we always had wild cherries, crab apple,
honeysuckle, locust. My father said, "We have enough
flowering trees."
I'm going to pour the wine down your throat, down
mine; I'll get us both drunk and stained bright
purple, dark blue with juice.

All because these seeds and saplings
were forbidden to me. I'd pay double the price
without desire.
All the time longing for wild-cherry trees
and the boundaries of my father's land, for my
mouth to be rinsed of the taste of you.

A Woman Picks Up the Habit of Anger

The astonishing knife-thrower grabbed my astonished hand,
shook it, invited me for a drink to get better acquainted.
We stayed for dinner, then grew intimate.

Anger became a casual thing: a slap on the shoulder,
a beating in the heart. I grew accustomed to the feel
of the bone handle, the edges of the other, steel end.

I never encouraged the arrangement. I was polite
but cold, properly dismayed. Anger played the razzle-
dazzle salesman on tour, the bus companion who jabbed me

in the ribs, told me jokes, broke my fists (I beat like
mad on the emergency windows, the door), ill-mannered,
vulgar, spilling vinegar on me at meals all the time,

presenting me with green eyes, a shiv of my very own—
valuable gifts. Nobody could resist a come-on like that,
so dark an invitation: the whirling disguises.

Brooding

I have a partridge egg,
a gift from a man
who found it in some field straw
near his home.

I find it every day in my own house
on a round, low table.
A bowl of envelopes sits beside it:
air-mail letters.

They go unanswered but are paper-thin,
crisp with intention.
They are red and blue with striped edges.
The egg is brown,
like sugar with drops of water on it,
speckled, and white.

Five years it's been on the same table.
I've never had a partridge.
Some years are fruitful and some aren't.
I could never tell.

The Only Child Sends a Gift to Her Mother

What came after me is the point—that one fall
night I arrived; an hour later the flowers; and never

another living child. I'm sorry to write it. Twenty-eight clever
years have come up with nothing between us. Even apart, I call

your late nights awake, the chrysanthemums on your table
the same as mine. Even from west to east, the change is
                                                    no hour.

This very instant, my night is in bloom with your sounds;
the same sleeping girl is asleep in the same cradle;

your amber mums sketch themselves on my white paper.
I believe these are only all your thoughts in my words,

secret as soil. Your back-yard backlit trees are what I've just
                                                    heard.
I write with your black pencil, not a second later.

Brecht Backstage: The Good Master

We hold out our paws toward feeling,
pad down the hall of reflections, barely
touching the red-coal floor.
Peg-leg Brecht burns straight through
to the stump; his hands could be brands
of forefinger arrows: "This way. See?"
We hold our paws out to feeling.

Or we ratchet like bears against fence posts,
trying for hide under fur too rough
to be got through: this burns, too.
Steelbrush Brecht goes straight to the heart
from the shoulder, rakes off the faked-up
pelts, yells, "Down to the *skin*. Did I almost
kill you?" Yes, you came too close not to.

Now the Heroine Weakens and Speaks

Now she buys new underclothes—buys new clothes—aptly
clothing herself in secret for any existing rival.
Already she has had a thought of elaborate flowers wrapped
in paper, laid just so at the door to a room, for her stunned
arrival.
Or of a dark-green bottle of sparkling wine, loudly uncapped—
and quite soon—as if marked doors were to pop wide open,
onto a blithe survival
for the great incipient duo, who, after all, at least began happy

just last week. The thing did begin in affection. Really, their eyes
in fact had met in agreement: several symmetrical looks of
sympathy, mapping
respective losses of loved, still lost antecedents. Dear Reader, I
have no idea why she would take this frail, feathery, free
creature, trap it
into that trained familiar (could it have been impatience?), or
what might
make her so unpainfully eager for all the inane display,
forgetful of right,
carelessly full of desire for the cast-off, ill-contrived trappings.

Two Bear

Oh, here.
Somebody's planted a white-shadowed cloud
on a deep-blue sky, and three tall trees beside it:
dark as can be under green-blue fir.

Who cares for being Linnaeus' subject?
The tall Latin *Felis,* the low *leo*—too many
names: and our *Ursa,* major and minor.

■

I would harm a fish, a fly—*pat-a-pum,* tapped down
by a quick swung paw—but I hope no man,
no further man.

■

Oh, other bear,
run up against a too live tree
and its fur-scratch knots—the rhythm of this
buzzing, humming, particular song,

do you know it? It's "Here, let me." Here, let me
step back just an inch to another place,
lumber toward being alive yet clean.

■

On a page somewhere, engraved with figures, our
character caught, we can never change. There is your
proper name, nature. There are your colored markings.

■

Look. Here.
Small blueberries in a small dirt bowl
that, one by one, take us up the hill
where they were the only nectar.

Small moving things: gold or gray, food
or fleas. Honey. And some wet smell somewhere,
like water, an unknown swimmer in a slow stream.

A Woman Kneeling in the Big City

I

AILANTHUS: DEMETER (ABOVE)
They think I have lost a coin, a beaded purse,
a miniature lover through the sidewalk grating—
hands and knees, string and a pin, and, worse,
calling to the underworld lord, "Return my daughter!"

But that's not it. One: There are trees down there,
palm-leafed sprays drawn up from smart, trapped seeds,
a new form of childhood marigold, unique and spare,
one paper cup out of thirty on a school windowsill.

This is no idyll. There are no pigeons lost
or wheeling through the stripy cellar-dark.
I have imagined nothing. And, of course, crisscross
iron bars let in the trash, tinfoil wrappers.

Two: The wind thunders up from the trains,
sound travels under the pavement. If the girl is gone,
a message will come through: "I am accompanied, brazen,
under trees, walking on coins. And oh, Mother, so are you!"

II

FIREWORKS: PERSEPHONE (BELOW)
The air down here is cool, springlike, black and green.
Trees rise like bamboo in a glass-walled atrium.
The young man silently papers a corner with warnings—
how war blossoms. You can hear wires humming

in the released steam. We sit at a makeshift table,
sometimes, planning the strategy that keeps me underground:
pomegranate seeds for pleasure. Surely my mother
is able to understand. I've come voluntarily down.

At other times, in the hollow, tiled caverns of empty stations,
where no trains run, we gather in excesses of noise—
brass-voiced "No more war"s, or firecrackers, or sighs
widening into anger. Overhead, before, I was not so impatient.

Now I boldly raise ladyfingers to my lips;
the exiled boulevardier strikes blue matches.
The fuses catch, the display burns under the gratings.
I throw the sparks higher—the pointed, committed kiss.

IN
COLOR

The Two Scenes in Color

1 FAR AWAY
Smelling of pinks, its light thrown crosswise as if through arches
but instead through trees—how this air here

turns what's white the color of sandstone or peaches.
And who gets taken in hand here? Me. How I'm spared

my "Where now?" and "How?" here. How the reach
for food has become a game. Watch the fruit: *Here. Higher.*

And shelter perches
at hand: parrot-green, canary-yellow—clear,

improbably pure, ordered. At night, the dark is all
struck matches, handclap lights, captive traces of sulfur,

and a choke-voiced dog set barking to guard old latches
makes no bones about fresh, instinctual fear.

2 HOME
Inside—this is where I hear drums,
and breathe in something like lemons.

First I think it comes from outdoors,
like our poor courtyard ragweed, earlier.

The noise is so quiet here you hear jets,
a single prop-plane propeller. West, the river

wets down the air, which comes here.
The drums, on a radio, pull a guitar

toward them. I believe I can recognize this.
The sky, on the way here, was thin

at the ends of streets:
gray pink, under salon-painterly

blue. Someone lifted the drums
from an old dark song. The lemons

have come from trees elsewhere—from a store.
Gold is the only way to see them: right there.

I Imagine Back

to the year when my throat, lungs, chest
were full of breath: hay mown into a haymow,
a field, a mulberry-treed roadside. Back
to precise black roads, starred and lettered
in unnamed weeds—in an arc: brown-gray
to goldenrod yellow, long-grass green,
and gray-brown.

How could I want to keep my heart
in this ignorance forever?

I imagine back to when coffee came
to take the first taste of its own name,
seeing at last its sweet, black,
true intention. A day when the woods,
like jobo wood, lay and begged to be freed
by the carpenter bird, making to measure
their own grain—the very beginning of myth

and prayer—though not that day inventing
the carpenter bird.

And finally back to the hour that started the
world, the start of me, when all things
alike were safe, alike at mercy,
and nothing but sharp-carved, living
fathers or mothers, ancestor gods,
trees, storms, had any will
or any power.

Though today I could nearly believe—
But no, it is not now so.

The Nearsighted

who misreads the serious joke, the speech
as everyday speech, the smile as pleasure, the map
as a flat land, sooner for later,

who once could misread "the law," briefly,
as "lawn party," longing perhaps
to see the great at leisure—the great

leisurely great at leisure on a lawn
in its late-summer greens, in their
black robes. No matter. Quickly corrected:

"the law." Takes off her glasses in spring
to see the flowers—*vide* Impressionists—light, air
in the National Arboretum. It is a mass, a confection

of colors, of course: a stroll in perfection. Solemnly
curling new hybrid tulips are only gaiety, planted in thrilling
profusion, variety. Purely a vision. One hill section

of overgrown lawn, beyond a hedge, holds twenty-odd columns
standing transplanted, standing alone, that hold no building.
Once they stood (a sign) at the first Capitol. Benefactions

saved them (a list of donors), to bring them here. Here
freestanding, mis-seen at a distance, the scene could be
scenery for an ancienter demos, dead grandeur. Close,

their Corinthian capitals cast such intricate shadows
down their sides—was it acanthus?—even the nearsighted sees
the Founders' stoneworker's first

intention, a far-off gesture: Yes, we chose
to believe this way. But now, here. The nation's given us
acres. Not so far away, the narcissus

garden, its near-hidden signs among short leaves, calls
for corrective lenses. It sends its instructive paths
through a polleny wood, telling us, "This

is Our Temple, among the gold-centered
namesakes of Presidents and First Ladies. . . . That's
the frilled Ring Leader. . . . Burning Heart. . . ." Thus

the bedazzled flower breeders, lovers of Beauty
all—romantics—giving names to what they admired, what
we had seen

as glorious, clean, benefaction. Not far off,

the tiny trees of the bonsai garden make each planting
a world. A nearsighted citizen finds six trees
in a foot-wide glade of beeches,

sees its minuscule guest, hears its minuscule
suppliants. Its invisible dryad: "This is pause
I give you, if I can—green hiatus

caught in a stone jar, just this far from magenta-
flowered truce in confusion, absurd azalea."
Foemina Juniper, white-dead branches spires

above a still-green forest—all just
inches tall—holds no natural fauna
the eye can see. The law

requires reason. Across a roadway, beds
of industrial herbs, medicinal herbs, et cetera,
smell as strong as sage. In the virtues of dittany

only the pungent, invisible gods believe. The
nearsighted sees bound water lilies in a popular pool
not far away, the civil golden carp

vague beneath them, and wants to believe there's no great
loss to be seen in this generation, no lost equilibrium, barely
a lost clear lost tradition.

Surface Tension

Desire restrained takes a long, cool bath,
indistinct at first in the blue water.

I make out a line of arm, a half-turned breast;
she slides down, runs the tap again, slides farther.

The bath is rippled porcelain, on cast iron,
with claws. A skylight catches sunlight. The room is bare.

This late-days hour was fired in a dry kiln.
Soap goes taut as boysenberries, around air.

No setting foot yet into the small room:
eyes only. Water any higher could do her harm,

or flood the checkered tiles too far beyond *eureka*.
Still, scattered fruit gathers on her raised arm.

Madrileña

1 WHAT'S FOREIGN
The word is *acacia*
when I mean "locust":
whatever this thin-leaved,
thick-flowered tall tree

might be, just outside
the front door. And *mora,*
dropping its presents,
must be "mulberry." Nobody

here knows the name for
what just lit on the wire
above the terrace, peeping,
trilling, then

singing its heart out.
I'd say "goldfinch,"
but I'd be wrong.
Drab yellow-green,

it's smaller than robins.
It lights, sings, then suddenly
flies to what's surely *olivo*.
Pájaro ("bird"), in any case.

The design of this place
is as it must be: not
for me—for the weather.
As every region has named

its food for the pot
it cooks in—*escudella*
or *pote, puchero*—touch
the wall in the shade,

is it cool as milk?
An aerial view like an agate
hangs on a whitewashed wall,
as a "You are here." This

is a lesson in somebody
else's passion—a lesson
in passion. Don't
romanticize. Just read.

2 WHAT'S INDIGENOUS
What were the words in the
hand-me-down sentence—
abecedario, wordbook—
and were there pictures?

A new, articulate Apple or Age,
a Blossoming Bed, a new Crown,
an old Dog come to a new house.
Even the Elder's a Fool here.

Consonant beings had long
since leapt into tenets:
consonant, copperbound
principles—code.

Whatever it was, I looked
to become it—as odd
as brass in a mold.
The ice-cold neck

of a jar of water,
cooling its contents right

in a hot sun: *jarra*.
Someone could say so.

Now water-light is cast on the ground
from higher windows, the present escaping
an *Ay* that I called *Ohh*.
This may be the odd memorial

just before the family forgets.
Just when I got here
the city was leaving,
a stationmaster

directing the crush
over the granite floors,
under the starry ceiling.
Twenty-four crowds

let their shirts brush—
strange for a nation.
Just when I'd learned the customs,
all new words were cut and healing.

By Daylight

In the tropical glass of a cool, foreign
mirror, I saw myself for the first time:
head forward on my unstraightened spine
from too much reading, cheeks scored

by impatience. I can never control
my eyes—gray, saddened at will,
with an uncurbed glare for looked-for double-dealing,
but still looking half a simpleton's after all.

And then, where the surface wavered,
I saw surprise—a sweating older woman, her coming
printed in faint lines around my mouth—and loved
the old bitch, whole, as if she were my next-door neighbor.

Proofreading My Father's Retina

I want to mark your eyes "Clean"
in the margin, let the printer
reset

your broken type; to focus your blurred
sight sharp as a clear, cold-colored
night.

No rip, no spot in the center or
off to the side, no damned
macula

in every scene. Your bad eyes
would stop their fearful
interference.

Let me try to help you mark them
for the lazy printer
"Clean."

Won't you try to examine daydreams
like night dreams, to see their
grammar

as if it were the glamour
of geysers contained in
geology,

as if you saw your self as your
daughter, you and non-you,
a language

foreign but spoken,
a joke shared and
gone?

Even in braille you could read
then as crazy saints read
scripture,

see as nursery birds see—straight
to the heart. Your more perfect,
or more

nearly perfect, knowledge, a
lesser sight, could still
start.

At the Creek Edge

So. Not a mystery anymore: the puffball spore,
puffed in a miniature puff—*poof*—out of the paper

sack of its owner and maker. What tribe or
nation was it who healed an infant's navel

with suchlike dust? A shake of its musty store
of cure and infant fungus exits, flies, sinks, wavers,

to cover the unavoidable hole. Only to us unclean,
perhaps: too black, perhaps, to be goodness

to someone like us. But off in the woods at evening
in childhood, touching a toe to puffballs half-hid in humus,

I saw them be brown and crumpled and black as just-retrieved
pages out of a fire. Readable dark-brown apples stood as

still as a still-life: you showed me how they blew their
life into the breeze at a blow, like somebody running, then

stopping. We stood at the creek edge—mother, dog,
                                        daughter—
showing or shown. Everything else around was red and yellow,
                                        dead

or dying; but they moved visibly, safe, into the coming year.
The stones under the creek were as round. The seed
                                                    would be fed

on dirt, air, water, elsewhere. No wonder you chose their image
for your grown-wild cells—poison but known, friendly—and
                                                            chose

to go pressing their dust into the air, so it could hang and
                                                        vanish
on the little bloodstream. Remember how faithfully the dog
                                                        showed,

sniffing through underbrush, under the gorgeous sumac—
pointing—where field mice lay? Remember how fast? How slow?

The Watches

1

Before they became mysterious and quartz, we longed to learn
the workings of watches: *eternal spring!* We knew
to rush to make time for things. Any delay
would make it too late. We knew
what the hands could say.

There was the timeless sculptor who took his time
with his block of stone, and made it smooth
as a stone. All the strange things we do
in actual fact adore
have become hard.

2

As on a gray-blue screen a stranger patiently sees
a soundless movie of her murmuring heart,
its valves too open or too shut, so
did a patron of his time's artisan
watch

the surface of a leaf-shaped dish—new, impatiently preened—
letting the loosened light through its gray-green jade
from the other side, and marvel at the useless care
of makers, but try to be careful: now the least
slippage meant downfall.

3

The minutes displayed and squared on a gray ground
slip from a 3 to an 8, a 9, without clicking.
They trip the alarm, however. It goes off
trilling its odd hour, telling its time
in church, or during a play.

The quiet halls of the city are famously full
of staggered peeping: half-hours, minutes—
seconds—from Standard Time. The place
sings with the fallibility in it.
That hasn't changed.

4

In the watches of the current night, some sickened
body steps up to look from a window, to see
an angle of river—a straight wet line
if whole. Anyone might get lost in
such a place, at such a time.

Now the city whistles to the worsened water, and attracts it.
The rivery haze in the air is so still a body can hear—
sharp-eared for ticking—every other person.
Each a confined or becalmed boat. No
one's loss makes another "free."

5

Of course the works have become complex. Still, time
works with its oldest tools, a lighted watchman
behind plate glass, heir to the laid-off soul
who lived in the watch-repair shop on
Spring Street.

What *is* it the quartz is doing in there? Responding
in seconds to the current of precise science,
just to enlighten us. We try to be glad
of knowing the truth, precise license,
so as not to please our misfortune.

A Translation of Love in Public

1

Everyone has sun-lighted rooms
and a time or two
that have decamped into the past year

or years. (In the place
next door, two fellows take in
the same pearl, and who knows what

that amazing laughter means. Or say
the aunt with the guitar arrives,
to build the new house, and look after

her sister's daughter: it's a strange island
that has cane burning and great, personable
clouds taking like paint to paper.)

Some of us drink beer, some drink red tea.
We can't stand the deadened senses.
This has become an oration.

We can't stand the deadened
senses or the oration.
Everyone has had sun-

lighted rooms decamp into the past
year or years. Everyone looks for them.
Everyone washes the windows

on a bright day. Everyone thinks
of washing the windows.
We like or don't like to hear stories

of sun-filled rooms. (That
window-red geranium trembling to the basement trains,
the painted sky; that loving laughter.)

We go buy music of the fullest kind
and buy drink and things to eat
from the basin of all that laughter.

There is bread, rice,
cake,
wine, water.

Everyone's had a small light room—
where death doesn't come—
proceed into the past year or years.

Everyone's had a moment of conception
all covered up in alarms and cries,
blankets and sirens.

Everyone's offered up the body to an everlasting
life. Everyone thinks of offering the body.
Some perhaps decide against it.

2
First, we had light
over a cracked sill.
Some food on the table.

Tavola? Mesa. Table.
How strange.
And coffee: *Caffè? Café.*

The tongues fall into agreement
in a schoolchild's game:
concordance, "to dance with the heart."

Listen.
The word falls onto its side
in the lighted dust

as if the floor were earth under the
sun, under a tangle of raspberry bushes
I was small enough to slide under.

You moved to turn
like a leaf to the light
when the light's come.

I closed my eyes.
Then it was dark.

3
Look.
In this sun-lighted room there is:
another language—*pa pa pi pi pe pe*.

Large books:
libri di parol e parole,
libros de palabras y palabras—

books of new words.
When I first learned your leaf-tumbled
ruin of tongues, I learned a new language:

yellow straw cut into a hot field,
cold wind in the olives. It was as if I'd
reseen this many-mouthed, poormouthed world

through your eyes—nation by nation.
But everyone at some time
has learned an ABC,

very small, a jewel of desire.
Everyone without exception wonders if
the world has in fact changed.

We Love It No End

The sun set again and again
as we came along the road to Madrid
from Valencia. It went down in
several ways: (1) So white it could not be
seen. It turned the hillocks before it
black: cut-carbon rises and falls
on a white ground. The blue-gray clouds
across it could have been black, too.
But, no, the hills were black.

Then, when they fell, it was different.
(2) Sign-neon rose. The sky all colors
we cannot speak of: a strung string
of deep-pink pearls. (3) With the clouds,
a true line of false horizon made a lake
of light in the mountains.
All these are things that we mustn't say.
The sprung plain making a rise
in the road before us, the sun
fell at every rise. *Robles,* oaks,

stood short against a faint-
bright sky—with the *chopos*/poplars
tall: *los álamos*. (4) The light-scalloped
edge of a dark cloud. The hills rose again
and covered it. Just when I thought
it had gone at last, we came
to a crest, it was there again,
in whatever color our new sky
chose to allow.